Ears of a Child

ISBN: 978-1-7337133-3-7

Published by NspireMe2B Publications
Birmingham, Alabama

Hi, my name is Jeniah. I am ten years old, and my little brother David is seven. We are homeschooled by our Mom. She teaches us all sorts of lessons for example, respect, love, and being thankful.

My Mom says she wants us to be the best we can be, and that the only way is to be obedient. Mom says she is to be a good example to us, and Dad is to do the same.

David and I learned something new this week. It all started when Mom sent us outside to play while she prepared dinner. She said, "Go out and play and I will call you back in once dinner is ready."

David and I went outside and ran around a bit. We started to play kickball while Daddy worked on the transmission of the family car.

We noticed every time he got something wrong, he would also get mad and would shout out words that did not seem appropriate for the ears of a child. David glanced over at Dad to see what was going on and we continued to play in the yard.

"Jeniah! Come inside to wash your hands and set the table." I ran in and did as Mom told me. I cleaned my hands with soap and water and then I set the table so that everyone would have their proper utensils to eat with.

After I finished, Mom called my little brother David and my Dad to come inside and wash their hands so that we can all eat together. They both ran in as if the food would disappear before they got inside. After everyone sat down, we said grace and we digged in.

At the dinner table, David could not stick his fork in his green peas. He tried and tried but did not succeed. It irritated him so much that one of the words Dad often used came flying out of his mouth.

It grew very quiet at the table; so quiet that you could hear a pin drop. David's eyes grew big as if he had seen a ghost. He was terrified.

"Son where did you learn that word?" Dad asked him, waiting for a reply.

"Well, I heard you say it a few times including a little while ago when you were working on the car, Daddy. Remember?"

Mom looked at Daddy, and Daddy's mouth dropped. He was very speechless at the Moment. I've never seen Dad so quiet before.

Mom explained, "David, you know you are not to use those type of words."

"But why not?" Asked David. "Daddy uses them all the time.

When I get older, I want to be like Daddy. Why can't I say the things that he says?"

David was confused. He held his head up with his little hand as he waited for an answer.

Mom and Dad looked at each other. Mom was disappointed because Dad used bad words in front of us, and Dad was disappointed in himself for letting Mom down.

Daddy said to David, "Well son, I was just a little angry and..."

"So can I say it when I am angry?" David asked while waiting for an answer.

Daddy had been put on the spot and was speechless once again. "No!" Mom quickly answered. "You can't use those words at all. Little boys do not speak those words, and little girls should not either. Now as for your Father, he will not be speaking inappropriate words again.

You should always respect yourself and others with what you are saying and doing." Once Mom finished speaking, her and I left from the table to leave the men there to think.

Everyone was shocked, especially me. But I understand that my Mom demands respect, and she wants the best out of us.

Daddy said, "Your Mom is right. I am going to make sure I set a better example."

David asked, "Are we going to wash our mouth out with soap, Daddy?"
"No son, we will just do what we know is right," Daddy replied. Daddy learned a valuable lesson today, and so did my brother David.

Mommy and I washed dishes together while Daddy and David cleaned the table and swept the floor.

Once we finished, we all sat down together and played games as a family.

Ears of a Child